NATIONAL GEOGRAPHIC

Can You See an Insect?

Felix James

Most insects are very small.

Most insects have enemies.
Their enemies like to eat them.

Some insects protect themselves from their enemies by hiding. Can you see an insect hiding here?

A grasshopper is hiding here.
This grasshopper is the same color as the bark.
Its color and shape help it hide from its enemies.

Can you see an insect hiding here?

A walkingstick is hiding here.
This walkingstick looks just like a twig.
Its color and shape help it hide
from its enemies.

Can you see an insect hiding here?

An inchworm is hiding here.
This inchworm looks just like the petals.
Its color and shape help it hide
from its enemies.

Can you see an insect hiding here?

A caterpillar is hiding here.
This caterpillar looks just like the leaves.
Its color and shape help it hide from its enemies.

Can you see an insect hiding here?

A katydid is hiding here.
This katydid looks just like the leaf.
Its color and shape help it hide from its enemies.

Index